A Choice T

MW00882181

Relationships

How To Get Along Better With The Important
People In Your Life

Kim Olver

From the "Choice Theory in Action" Series

ISBN: 9781072472995

First Published by Amazon, June 2019

Dedication

This book is dedicated to my two sons, Dave and Kyle, and the beautiful, inside and out, women they chose for life partners and mothers of my eight grandchildren. They gave me purpose and meaning after my husband, their father, died and now they are shining examples of healthy relationships. They are providing excellent examples for their children to learn invaluable relationship skills to serve them throughout their lives.

CONTENTS

The Choice Theory In Action Series

This is one of a series of short books aimed at helping people gain better control of their lives using ideas from Choice Theory psychology, a theory of human behaviour that was developed by Reality Therapy creator Dr. William Glasser.

In this selection of books we explain the application of Choice Theory psychology to a range of popular themes such as Addiction, Anger, Depression, Happiness, Parenting, Relationships, and Stress. The authors are all experts in Choice Theory psychology and all have studied directly under its creator, Dr. William Glasser.

The author, Kim Olver, has written several books where she applies the ideas of Choice Theory to relationships and the breadth and depth of her experience shows in her writing. As he grew in age and wisdom Dr. Glasser reached the conclusion that healthy relationships were vital to personal happiness and this book offers the reader a fresh view of relationships from a Choice Theory perspective.

Brian Lennon
Series Editor

Acknowledgements

It is impossible to write a book about Choice Theory without expressing deep gratitude to Dr. William Glasser who created this psychology that has literally changed my life, both personally and professionally. It makes so much sense to me and allows me to make sense of the world and the people in it.

I would also like to thank my Choice Theory instructors, Nancy Buck, Peter Appel, Al Katz, Martin Price, Art Sheil, Liz Tham, Rhon Carleton, the late Karen Sewall and Pierre Brunét.

I'd like to thank the Choice Theory people who trust me enough to bring me to their countries, schools, businesses and organizations to train: Brian Lennon, Annabelle Symes, Glasser Australia, Boba Lojk, Dubravka Stijačić, Clare Ong, Anasuya Jegathevi Jegathesan, Scott D'Alterio, Kristina Kraus, Steve Hammond, Brian Patterson, Sue Tomaszewski, Web Eberwein, Dave Betz, Lisa Thompson, Regina Fike, Tom Callahan, Nano Farabaugh, Rachel McElroy, Lois DaSilva-Knapton and Les Triché.

I want to thank the Board of William Glasser International for doing the challenging job of carrying on after Dr. Glasser's death. It is not easy to steer a rudderless ship, but with Brian Lennon and John Cooper's capable captaining, the organization is going strong and will continue to grow even stronger.

Because Choice Theory is such a relationship-oriented psychology, I have made many friends through the work. Those friends all deserve my thanks, not just for their friendships—although that is enough—but also challenging me to grow, learn more and take Choice Theory to greater heights. It is through teaching that I learn and grow the most. There are way too many to mention. Even if I made a valiant attempt, I am certain I'd leave someone important out. You know who you are. Thank you my friends!

I want to thank my team: Denise Daub, Crystal Alston, Veronica Daub and Sheri Macewko, who keep me going while making it look easy. I couldn't do what I do without you.

Last but certainly not least, I also want to thank my two sons, Dave and Kyle, and their wives, Stacey and Jesse, and my eight grandchildren of Olvers: Saige, Zavier, Logan, Emerson, Maeson, Perry, Mallory and Lincoln. Their love and support is immeasurable. I'm sure they would prefer me to be in Pennsylvania with them, spending more time with the children, but, as my son Kyle said on a recent visit, "I know your work is important; you help a lot of people." My children have always supported me in my quest to share the messages of living a happier, more satisfying life. They live better lives because of Choice Theory and know of my passion for bringing it to as many people as I can.

1. Setting the Scene

There is a known phrase, often proclaimed at weddings: "And two shall become one." It's a lovely, romantic sentiment, but does it truly manifest in real life? How can two people become one? Personally, I've never seen it happen, and I'm a true romantic at heart.

Whether it is friendship, familial, work-based, or an intimate connection, two people are two people. When they decide to enter a relationship, they remain two people.

This can make finding harmony within a relationship difficult. Let's examine some of the many ways two people can be different.

People may have incompatible need profiles. They may want different things. They enter relationships with different life experiences and discrepant learning bases. People have different value systems or, at the very least, a different hierarchical arrangement of values.

The aspects of ourselves that make us unique provide the elements of a perfect storm for disharmony in our relationships.

We now know from advances in neuroscience that the human brain is hardwired for negativity. We notice most when things aren't right and we aren't getting what we want. This explains how something trivial can become so enormous in relationships. With our focus fixated on the things we *don't* like, the myriad of things we *do* like is often forgotten, neglected, or relegated to the background of our lives.

In addition to these internal building blocks of our personality and behavior, there are also many outside factors: religion, politics, relatives, friends, finances, and other influences that can test the strength of any relationship. With all these factors, is it any wonder the divorce rate is 53 percent in the U.S.? Of those 47 percent that remain, a good bit of them are unhappy, frustrated and resentful that they didn't get the 'happily ever after' they were expecting.

Once people recognize they're not getting what they want, people tend to engage in methods of external control to change the situation into something more in their favor.

There are four versions of external control and none of them are helpful to relationships:

1. You're trying to get me to do something I don't want to do,

2. I'm trying to get you to do something you don't want to do.

3. We are each trying to get the other to do something neither of us wants to do.

4. I am trying to do something I don't want to do primarily to please you.

You may be thinking, isn't that what people do in relationships? And I would answer yes, many times, that is what people do. But is it inevitable? The unequivocal answer to that question is no!

The alternative is to listen and learn from each other in order to give and receive information that will help you choose a different path—a path toward supporting, appreciating and celebrating each other despite your differences and, ultimately, because of your differences.

2. Choice Theory Psychology

Dr. William Glasser, a world-renowned psychiatrist, developed the concept of Choice Theory psychology. It began as an explanation of all human behavior before developing into a form of counseling, guiding people toward understanding the external control beliefs and behaviors they hold and engage in. Finally, Choice Theory morphed into a way of living life: practicing internal control and the Connecting Relationship Habits, which will be elaborated on in Chapter 10.

Without exception, Choice Theory psychology can be used to explain why anyone does anything. Every person is always choosing the best behavior they have available to them, at any given point in time, with the information available to them, to get something they want. You may not be able to look from the outside and know what the other person wants, but behavior is no longer a mystery. The behavior you see is the person's best attempt to get what he wants.

Basic Needs

Choice Theory begins by discussing the five basic human needs. We all have the same needs and Choice Theorists teach that these needs, and their corresponding individual strengths, are genetically determined. All people have these five basic needs in common, but how strongly we experience each of them is determined by genetics and the circumstances we find ourselves in.

While the predetermined strengths of these needs do not change over time, a smaller need will take priority if it's being neglected or if we are in a situation where it is harder to get that need met. We feel best when our needs are satisfied to the degree we want them to be without having too little or too much.

Unfortunately, our genetic instructions didn't come with gauges that tell us how strong and satisfied each need is at any given point in time, so we must rely on our general feelings of satisfaction, happiness and peace. When we experience those things, we know our needs are being met. When we are having a different experience, it is up to us to determine which need is out of whack and what to do about it.

The basic needs of Choice Theory psychology are Survival, Power, Love & Belonging, Freedom and Fun. I sometimes call the need for Power, Significance; the need for Love & Belonging, Connection; and the need for Fun, Joy. I find these words more encompassing than the original.

People with a high Survival need tend to prioritize safety over everything else, avoid risky behavior and worry a lot, particularly about the people in their life who are risk-takers. They are health conscious, often prioritizing things like exercise, eating healthy and getting enough rest. They like to plan for every contingency, prefer saving to spending and plan for the long-haul rather than engaging in spontaneous activity.

Those with a high Power need prioritize respect over most things. They value recognition and tend to feel frustrated without it, particularly if it's deserved. It is important to them to make a difference and have an impact. They like to win, be correct and have the last word in an argument. It is imperative to leave a legacy. People with a high Power need like to be in control of what is happening around them, and they are constantly updating the skills that are important to them.

People with a high Connection need like spending time with other people. They like to help others and often take on the peacemaker role; when it comes to their personal situations, they're typically conflict-avoiders. Giving and receiving love is their favorite thing to do. They are generally highly in tune with others, being able to sense when something is wrong, or if someone is upset about something. Their relationships are deep, meaningful and never superficial. People with a strong need for Connection prioritize people over everything else, even themselves.

Those with a high Freedom need tend to like doing what they want above all else. They are frustrated with feeling restricted and having limited options; they prefer time alone over time with others. They tend to be fiercely independent, sometimes making decisions that aren't in their best interest just to do the opposite of what someone told them to do. They deeply value their privacy and question rules, fighting constantly against the status quo. People with a high Freedom need tend to be highly creative and think outside the box.

Those with a high need for Fun/Joy prioritize Joy over everything else. In fact, they tend to avoid anything they perceive as being without joy. They have a great sense of humor, love to laugh and enjoy making others laugh. Those high in Fun/Joy tend to seek learning opportunities for the joy of discovery and prioritize relaxation and play.

It is important to note that everyone is influenced by all five needs; each need exists in our need-strength profile, but one or two typically act as the motivation for many of our behaviors.

Your need-strength profile is a graph depicting each of your five basic needs and their corresponding strengths. Based on how your unique need-strength profile manifests, certain things in our life are perceived as need-satisfying and feel very, very good. It is impossible to predict what is need-satisfying to someone else, but for yourself, you know when something meets one or more of your basic needs when it ends up being stored in what Choice Theory calls our Quality World.

Quality World

When you experience things in life as extremely pleasurable that meet at least one or more of your basic needs of Survival, Love & Belonging, Power, Freedom and Fun, then you will store it—whether it be a person, place, object, behavior, belief, or value —in your Quality World. This is a magical place, as everything is perfect there. If you could live a life filled with all the things in your Quality World, you would be happy all the time. But alas, we are forced to cope with the reality of our lives, which often falls short of the perfection within our Quality World.

It is important to note that not everything in our Quality World will match society's definition of quality. Smokers typically have cigarettes in their Quality World, child perpetrators have child abuse and batterers have domestic violence in theirs.

There is no conscience in the Quality World… it is simply filled with those people, places, things, behaviors, beliefs and values that feel extremely good to the individual and meet one or more of the five basic needs. Even though they haven't been experienced, hopes, dreams and fantasies can live in the Quality World. When experienced, they either become solidified as a Quality World picture or, if the experience didn't meet expectations or interest was lost, they leave the Quality World.

Comparing Place

Our waking hours are spent focused on something we want in our Quality World, while searching our perceptions of whether there is a match for what we want. When there is a match, it feels good; when there isn't, it's painful. Even when we have what we want, it isn't 100% positive. There is typically a tradeoff we need to experience to get what we want. A promotion at work often comes with increased responsibility and less leisure time. Becoming a couple may be what you want, but it brings a decrease in freedom. Having a child may be what you want but brings a corresponding increase in responsibility and a decrease in expendable income. There's always a tradeoff.

Similarly, when you aren't experiencing what you want and it feels painful, there is always a benefit, even if you don't realize it at the time. Our painful experiences provide gifts, lessons and opportunities (GLO) if only you have the mind to search for them.

Once you have determined if you have a match for what you want, you move into a place where you assess what behavioral options are available for you to either maintain what you want, obtain what you want, or focus on getting something else that you want.

Behavioral System

Your behavioral system is the place where possible behavioral options are stored. This includes all the behaviors you have ever used in the past, whatever new behaviors you may think of and, sometimes, even subconscious behavioral choices you aren't aware of.

When looking for your next, best behavior, you will always choose what you believe is the best behavior available to you at that time to get what you want.

Total Behavior

Out of everything Choice Theory contributes to the field of psychology, the concept of total behavior is what Glasser was most proud of. Choice Theory claims that every behavior is comprised of four inseparable component parts: actions, thoughts, emotions and physiology. These parts occur simultaneously and are in sync with one another. If you don't believe it, try a simple exercise.

Stand up and adopt a slumped posture; looking at your feet, think of something you don't like and say in your best Eeyore voice, "I'm so happy!" Are you feeling happy? Of course not! Now try the opposite. Stand up with your head up, shoulders back, and think of something you like. Throw your arms in the air, jump and exclaim excitedly, "I'm so depressed!" How are you feeling? Your emotions will match the rest of your behavior.

Thinking of the four components—actions, thoughts, emotions and physiology—it is obvious that we can only directly control our actions and, with practice, our thoughts. If you want to change the way you are feeling or how your body is responding, you would want to change what you are doing or thinking to get the corresponding change in emotion and physiology.

As you enact the total behavior, you are trying to get the world to look more like your Quality World so you can more effectively meet your needs. This is a loop that continues all day long, every day of your life.

3. How CT Applies to Relationships

Choice Theory recognizes how challenging it is for two people, with their own individual perceptions, wants and needs, to create a peaceful life together.

Choice Theory knows that the Quality World of both individuals is strong; people want and need different things. Add to that the fact that everyone has their own unique perceptions of the world based on their focus, knowledge, experiences and values, and it's a wonder two people can build a life together at all.

For two people to have a successful relationship, from a Choice Theory perspective, each person must be willing to prioritize the needs and wants of the relationship over their individual needs.

Choice Theory also teaches that everyone is doing the best they know in any given situation with the information available to them to get what they want. If this is clearly understood and internalized, there is no reason to complain, blame or criticize the other person. Why would you criticize someone for doing the best he or she can?

It is important to avoid taking your partner's behavior personally. It is rare that a person is behaving just to upset you. It is much more likely that they are behaving to get something they want to satisfy the needs that are most salient at that time.

Dr. William Glasser developed a process called, "Structured Reality Therapy," to be used only with couples who really want their relationship to work. Too often, couples come to therapy after they have done so much damage to each other that they have little left to work with.

When couples are in distress, "Structured Reality Therapy" asks five questions. The job of the person speaking is to speak their truth; the job of the person listening is to listen for genuine understanding—not just to hear the other person, but to do their best to see the problem from their partner's eyes.

The therapist asking the questions will serve as a referee to ensure the party listening is doing their task without interrupting the other or defending themselves. The therapist will redirect the person back to their job of listening to understand their partner.

If you believe your partner wouldn't want to participate in a Structured Reality Therapy session, you can go through the process on your own. This also works well if your goal is to surprise your partner with a behavior to improve the relationship. Give it a whirl and imagine your partner's answer to the questions. Then, decide to commit to implementing your answer for number five without requiring any change from your partner.

Here are the questions:

1. Are you here because you really want help with your relationship?

This question is to eliminate those who are in therapy to just check the box before opting for separation or divorce. It is also asked to determine if one person is interested and the other isn't. If the couple is ready for divorce, no amount of therapy is going to help. If one person wants to fix the relationship and the other doesn't, then it's time for individual therapy with the one who is most unhappy with the relationship. When both people are interested in fixing the relationship, then "Structured Reality Therapy" is a more than a viable option.

2. Whose behavior can you control?

This question is asked so that if someone is insistent that the other person must change, the therapist can remind him or her: you can only control your own behavior. Insisting someone must change to fix your problem does not work. A person may decide to change because he or she is prioritizing the relationship, but forcing someone to change rarely produces a change that lasts.

3. Tell me what you see as the problem in your relationship?

This question offers the couple a chance to release all the complaints they have collected over the years. To provide a bit of insulation, the person venting will address their partner in the third person and direct the complaints to the counselor, making it easier for the other person to listen.

4. **Tell your partner what is right in the relationship. Why do you want to fix it?**

After listening to each partner's list of complaints, the counselor asks each person to tell the other what they value about the other person and their relationship. This important step is to help each person remember why they've decided to participate in counseling. They want to fix the relationship—why? What is it about each other they value? The couple will take time to share this with each other so they can be reminded of and experience the positive feelings they have for each other.

5. **After listening to what your partner likes and what they don't, what are you willing to do every day this week to improve your relationship?**

This question is asked so each person will choose the thing *they* think is best, that *they* are willing to do, to help the relationship. The therapist doesn't make suggestions nor is either person permitted to ask for what they want. The idea is that each person heard the complaints and the things the other person likes and appreciates. Now they can choose to stop doing something that bothered their partner, start doing or increase something their partner appreciates, or choose a behavior that wasn't mentioned that the person thinks will be most helpful to the relationship. When the decision to behave is made internally rather than having it requested externally, it is more likely to be followed without resentment.

Typically, after a week of working daily to improve the relationship, the couple has moved significantly closer to each other. If the therapist assesses the couple is ready, either now or in subsequent sessions, he or she teaches the couple about the Solving Circle, which you will learn about in Chapter Nine.

Another unique application of Choice Theory to relationships involves the use of the Connecting Relationship Habits. These will be discussed in Chapter Ten.

4. Who Owns the Problem?

Couples often come into therapy with a clear idea of where the fault lies in the breakdown of their relationship, and it isn't within themselves. There is a lot of finger pointing in couples' therapy, but practicing Choice Theory puts an end to that quickly.

It really doesn't matter whose fault it is. What is most important is whose responsibility it is to fix it, and deciding if it's worth trying to repair the damage external control has caused in the relationship.

For people who don't understand Choice Theory, this can be a difficult to accept. It's much more satisfying to be the victim and have people in your life rally around to support you in dealing with the problems your partner is creating. However, the person who is most upset about the relationship is the one who owns the problem and is therefore the one responsible for its solution.

As a relationship counselor, I have heard some common, mundane problems among couples that could be easily solved by the person taking responsibility for the problem and its ultimate solution. Two such everyday problems that are simple, yet common, involve leaving dirty clothes on the floor instead of in the hamper and allowing the fuel to get so low in the car that the low fuel indicator illuminates the dashboard.

The person complaining about the clothes on the floor points a finger at the perpetrator. While it is true the other person is the perpetrator, the owner of the problem is the person most upset about it: the non-offender. Similarly, the person upset about the gas light on the dash of the car blames their partner for not getting gas, but the truth is, the one complaining is most upset and, therefore, owns that problem.

Once problem ownership is ascertained, the right person can begin to take responsibility for the solution. In the case of the clothes, the non-offending person could simply bend over, pick up the clothes and put them where he or she wants them. In the case of the fuel, the person concerned about their partner running out of fuel could jump in the car, take it to the gas station and fill it up. In each case, problem solved!

The challenge occurs when people try to externally control their partners into realizing the problem is really theirs and they should change to make the bothered person's life better. This approach rarely works to fix the problem because people who leave clothes on the floor or let their low fuel indicator turn on are doing so because it meets their needs.

In relationships, a lot could be solved by learning that other person is not engaging in their 'offensive' behavior just to bother you. People do what they do to get something they want that they believe will more effectively meet their needs—it isn't personal. The one leaving clothes on the floor isn't thinking, "I know what I can do to really upset my partner today..." And people don't drive by the gas station thinking, "I'm just going to skip getting gas tonight so I can frustrate my partner. That will be fun."

Once you understand your partner isn't doing these things *to* you, you are free to see the real motivation for their behavior. Perhaps your partner wants to hurry into bed to cuddle with you, so the clothes go on the floor and he or she doesn't leave enough time in the morning to pick them up. Maybe the one with a low fuel tank is hurrying home to cook dinner or to take the kids to some after school activity and realizes he or she will have more time in the morning to stop for gas. You may not agree, but the person isn't responsible for meeting your needs; they are responsible for meeting their own needs, which is exactly what they are doing.

Figure out what you need to do to fix your problem so you can stop expecting your partner to change his or her behavior to suit you.

These examples are relatively inane, but this process will work for any problem.

5. Effective Communication

When I did the research for my book *Secrets of Happy Couples*, I discovered four factors happy couples identified as their success factors, with one of them being communication. I never use the word communication without prefacing it with 'effective' because, in many couples, there is a lot of communication going on, but it isn't always effective.

What makes communication effective? It's when both people are communicating in ways that the other person can understand. Too often in relationships, we listen to our partner just long enough to take something personally, get defensive, or make a judgment about what was said that isn't accurate.

We often "read between the lines" of what our partner says without taking the time to really understand. Listening for understanding is a high-level skill which requires the listener to hear what the other person is saying without becoming upset, angry, or trying to argue the person out of the points he or she making.

Another part of communication that can go awry is our nonverbal communication. You may be quite adept at saying the 'right' things, but if your nonverbal behavior doesn't match up, an astute partner will notice the difference and put more stock in your nonverbal behavior rather than your words.

For instance, when you are agreeing with your partner while shaking your head from side-to-side. That will be interpreted more as a disagreement rather than an agreement.

When you ask your partner if they really are 'fine' with what you just discussed, and your partner is answering with clipped tones and has his or her arms folded in front of their body, this will often be interpreted as the opposite of 'fine.'

Some people are better at reading the nonverbal cues than others, which can result in a huge misunderstanding. Your wife is saying everything is fine, but you don't notice her nonverbal cues telling you it isn't, so you move forward thinking she is in agreement. Later when she's furious and you are confused, you may think back and realize you missed some nonverbal language.

It can be difficult to listen for understanding when you are simultaneously feeling attacked, which can happen if you are being told you are the object of your partner's unhappiness. It's easier to do when the communication involves something else.

One challenge in the communication arena is that women tend to speak 20,000 words in a day while men speak 7,000. This information comes from a study the Daily Mail reported on, "Women Talk Three Times as much as Men, Says Study." You can search for it there.

From this information, women will deduce they are better communicators and men will declare women talk too much! There is something about the human condition that helps us believe our way is the 'right' way. When you begin a communication exchange with a bias against your partner, it is difficult to listen for understanding.

Listening for understanding does not mean you must agree with your partner; you can understand where they are coming from and still see things differently. Listening for understanding involves holding space for each person to have different experiences, perceptions and beliefs and realizing it's not your job to conquer your partner by getting him or her to think the same way you do. The YouTube video "Perceptions: shower curtain" is a great illustration of this concept.

This is the first step in listening for understanding, but it isn't the last: you can recognize you have different opinions and still dismiss the opinion of your partner. When listening for understanding, you are doing your best to see the world through your partners eyes. You are imagining what the world is like for your partner, which may include temporarily suspending your worldview.

This is becoming increasingly obvious in the #MeToo Movement. Men and women are often on opposite sides of this issue. It's difficult for some men to imagine how women are sexually assaulted in such high numbers. They may have experienced sexual manipulation by women, making it hard to see them as a victim. If they are men who would never assault a woman, it's difficult to imagine their friends and family members as men who might. As a woman, it can be difficult to hear the men in her life badmouthing women and suggesting she probably did it voluntarily to get ahead in her job, regrets it now and calls it sexual assault. These and more are examples of conversations that are happening around the world.

It is not to say there aren't many men who support the movement, but the recent controversy over the January 2019 Gillette commercial makes it obvious there is a lack of listening for understanding surrounding this issue. This isn't even an issue that is likely personally affecting the couples' relationship unless one of them had been assaulted or accused, but it's an interesting example of what divides us: It's not just gender, but race, politics, religion and more.

Even though it's difficult for a man to imagine what life is like for a woman and vice versa, it's necessary when you are attempting to listen for understanding. What's most important is that the effort is being made.

If you are committed to effective communication, then you need to speak in ways your partner can understand by avoiding accusations, criticism and emotionally-charged topics. Instead, be careful how you speak so your partner can listen instead of reacting by taking offense to your words or tone. The listener needs to put themselves in the place of the other person in order to effectively imagine the world from that person's point of view. This involves not jumping to conclusions, becoming defensive and going for the attack. When those tendencies come up, remind yourself to be curious instead of judgmental so you can truly understand your partner's position.

When couples communicate effectively, particularly during difficult topics and stressful times, their relationships become stronger and they report greater satisfaction in it.

6. Creating Shared Quality World Pictures

While we all have and experience the same five basic needs in varying degrees, it is our Quality World pictures that motivate our behaviors. When you think of all the things you think you *need*, if it isn't Survival, Love & Belonging, Power, Freedom and Fun, then whatever you believe you need is actually something you *want*. There is a world of difference between what you want and what you need. Proclaiming that you "absolutely *need* coffee" really means you "*want* to have coffee."

Remember that romanticized notion that two individuals become one once they get married? Marriage does not make two individuals one person. Conversely, a committed relationship will accentuate the differences between two individuals. Everyone is influenced by where they place their focus, their life experiences, and their values, which forms their own unique perceptions.

As individuals live their lives, they develop their own personal nirvana called the Quality World discussed in Chapter Two. That is where things, people, places, values and beliefs that satisfy their needs and comprise perfection for that individual are stored. Usually people in a relationship have some shared Quality World pictures. Often, liking and enjoying some of the same things is something that you're attracted to in another person. This would represent a shared Quality World picture.

If you are to continue to keep your relationship fresh and exciting, it's a good idea to continue to develop shared Quality World pictures. Brian Lennon, a Choice Theory instructor in Ireland says, "People are happy if most of their needs are met most of the time. A relationship is happy if most of its needs are met... and that means achieving shared pictures."

In the beginning of a relationship, it is a joy to discover and delight at the pictures you share. As you commit to a relationship with one another, it is important to spend time together engaging in shared Quality World pictures. It is also important to continue to have novel experiences together which help to create even more Quality World pictures to share.

Toward that end, it is important to continue to have dates, take vacations to the extent you are able and try new things together. The examples of what couples may enjoy together can stretch out to infinity: talking walks; eating at their favorite restaurant or trying new places; visiting family or friends; taking cooking, dancing, or painting classes; taking a drive to a new place; being on or near the water, mountains, or city; going to a live event; having tea.

Pretty much anything two people can do simultaneously is a possibility as long as you both like the outcome. You won't always have a match but, along the way, you can enjoy wonderful adventures, create great memories and strengthen your relationship by discovering and creating more shared Quality World pictures with each other.

7. Expectations

I love this quote by Kyle Cease: "No one ever broke your heart; they broke your expectations." It blows my mind with its honest simplicity. Choice Theory helps us understand how important trust is in a relationship, but trust comes in many forms. We can ruin a relationship by trusting a person to be who we want them to be instead of who they actually are.

Expectations are what drives that problem. We expect our loved ones to act and think the way we imagine they do in our Quality World. When they don't, we either apply a lot of pressure to get them to conform—feeling angry or depressed to punctuate our dissatisfaction—or we choose to leave the relationship physically, mentally, or emotionally. It is rare that people can accept they are holding higher standards than their human has ever achieved and are simultaneously blaming them for not fulfilling their expectations. Does this sound as crazy to you as it does to me? It may be crazy, but it's also incredibly common.

What's the answer then? No expectations at all? It is perfectly acceptable to have expectations for yourself, unless you are a perfectionist. If you have the expectation that you must do everything to perfection, you have doomed yourself for a brokenhearted existence. No one can be perfect all the time at everything they attempt—sometimes people must settle for just good enough. Holding expectations short of perfection in your important areas can be highly motivating as you spend your days attempting to keep upping your own personal best. The question you would continue to ask is, "Am I better today than I was yesterday?"

Holding expectations of others may give you a false sense of security as you say to yourself, "My loved one would never do that!" However, you don't know that. There's no guarantee your partner will conform to what you think of him or her, or to a behavior he or she has demonstrated in the past. Life has a way of happening, causing us to reorganize our priorities.

Sometimes promises go unfulfilled. Haven't you ever had to break a promise that when you made it, you were sure you would be able to keep? Of course, you have. Everyone does, unless you go through life without making promises. You won't be able to escape the promises though that loved ones infer from your silence. When you promise nothing, loved ones tend to fill in the blanks, believing you are promising something you will later deny and feel justified in your denial. They will feel equally justified in their assumptions.

Expectations abound in relationships. Your partner expects you to take out the trash on Thursday, to brush the snow off your car in the winter and to never, ever engage in flirtation with a member of the opposite sex. You expect your partner to always be available for sexual activity at any time, to do the grocery shopping and be the liaison for the school in all things pertaining to your children. Everything is fine provided everyone complies with the expectations, but when something changes and a person prioritizes other commitments, be ready for some serious fallout!

I have an answer to this pitfall of relationships: The Unconditional Trust Challenge. I started it in September of 2017, thinking I would do it for 30 days, but I like the freedom it gives me so I have decided to adopt it for life. I encourage anyone else who would like to join me to make the commitment.

In the Unconditional Trust Challenge, you trust everyone. You trust everyone to do what Choice Theory tells us they will already do—no broken promises, no need to take anything personally. You will trust everyone to do the best they can to get what they want in their situation with the information available to them at that point in time. When you care about someone, isn't that what you want them to do?

The problem comes when someone important to you is doing something to get what *they* want and it makes getting what you want more difficult or even impossible. Don't you have a right to be hurt or angry then? Of course, you can feel disappointed, hurt and angry, but is that how you want to feel?

I know I don't particularly like feeling that way and, since I've learned Choice Theory, I don't *have* to feel those emotions for very long and neither do you! When you remember the other person is doing the best they can to get what *they* want, not necessarily what *you* want, you can be more accepting of the reality of their choices.

I'm not talking about stuffing those feelings away or living in denial of the experience; I'm talking about changing your thoughts, so your feelings also change. When you think things like, "it's not fair," "You promised, "I can't believe I trusted you," "You are such a horrible person," "I can't have what I want with you doing that," those emotions are inevitable. They coincide with and accompany those thoughts. Instead tell yourself, "I had hoped you were going to do this, but since you are doing something else now, I will figure out how to get what I want in this situation." You have many options.

Imagine your friend was going to take you to the theatre but decided instead he needed to spend time with his friends playing softball. Naturally, you would be disappointed, but when you trust your friend to make the best decision for himself, you might want to be happy for him. Now your task is to decide among the options available to you: you can stay disappointed and miserable, you can ask another friend to go with you, you can go alone, or you could decide to do something else enjoyable. It's as simple as answering the question, "Who do I want to be in this situation?"

Once you commit to the Unconditional Trust Challenge, you understand that each one of us lives our lives doing the best we can to get the most of what we want. Even when you do things selflessly for others, you are really matching the picture you have in your Quality World of yourself as a helpful, loving person. When you accept the responsibility of meeting your own needs and stop expecting others to do that for you, you become a whole person, capable of being happy regardless of what is happening around you. This gives you such an attractive energy; others will want to spend time around you in hopes to get something of what you have.

The flip side of taking responsibility for meeting your own needs is that you also allow others the freedom to meet theirs as they see fit, and you stop falling into the trap of believing that you can meet their needs for them.

When you are in a healthy relationship, both people are capable of meeting their own needs and they also prioritize the relationship, in turn providing opportunities for the other person to get his or her needs met within the relationship. Two people don't become one. Two healthy individuals become a couple when they are already whole and need nothing from the other person except to share in the experience of life. It's a beautiful thing.

Join the Unconditional Trust Challenge and find out how wonderful it can be!

8. Negotiating for the Win/Win/Win

When I speak at US Army Yellow Ribbon events for Army members who have served overseas and their family members, I speak about a concept they call 'battle mind.' When you are on a mission, you must be intensely focused on accomplishing that mission and nothing else. It doesn't matter if your husband or wife just sent you divorce papers, you learned your grandmother just died, or that your child was suspended from school for carrying a weapon; you don't have the luxury of thinking about it during a mission. You are required to compartmentalize whatever is bothering you so you can be 100% focused on accomplishing the objective. This serves soldiers well in battle, but what do you think it does when you adopt this mindset for negotiating differences with the important people in your life?

Most of us have 'battle mind' whenever we enter any negotiation. We aren't concerned with what the other person wants; we are only concerned that we get what we want. We want to win. This is our Power need at work.

When you begin a negotiation, you are already an expert at one thing—your position. You do not need to spend a lot of time honing your position.

However, the part you do need help with is understanding the position of the other person.

When you negotiate differences, you want to first listen to the other person to learn what it is he or she wants. Don't stop listening if it isn't immediately what you want or if it seems to threaten that. Don't take it personally or think the other person is trying to ruin your plans. Remind yourself that you are two separate people who sometimes want different things, but when you work at negotiating, you will be able to reach a solution that will work for the both of you. Engage Stephen Covey's principle from his book, *7 Habits of Highly Effective People* to, "Seek first to understand, then to be understood."

Let's say you and your partner only get one week vacation a year so you sit down to plan your next one. You want to go to the Star Hotel and your partner wants to go to the Ritz. Initially, this caused some tension and even a bit of bickering. But when that got you nowhere, you decided to try a new tact.

You began to listen to one another to gain better understanding. Upon further exploration, you learn that your partner wants to go to the Ritz because it's in the mountains, whereas you want to go to the Star because it's close to the beach. With this better understanding, you realize the crux of the situation: one of you wants to go to the beach and the other wants to go to the mountains. What can you do? You could find a location with both. You could take turns, go to the mountains this year and the beach next year. Maybe you spend three days at the beach, travel a day, and spend three days in the mountains. Perhaps you choose an alternate location you both agree on as a second choice, such as a cabin in the woods by a lake. You could take two long weekends in each location. You could decide on a staycation so you could save your money to take that Alaskan cruise you've been wanting to take. Once you make your goal finding a solution that is agreeable to both parties, you have established a win/win/win—you win, your partner wins and the relationship wins by going through the process.

9. Prioritizing Something Bigger than Yourselves

Another one of the four self-proclaimed secrets for success I discovered while researching for my book, *Secrets of Happy Couples*, is prioritizing something bigger than yourself. Some people mentioned a Higher Power or the relationship itself as the thing that was bigger than themselves. Prioritizing what your Higher Power might want you to do or what is best for your relationship *most* of the time—because no one can do it *all* the time—goes a long way in improving the health of the relationship.

If you are an individual with a high Freedom need and no Connection need, it would be difficult to prioritize something bigger than yourself. The Freedom need is about unlimited restriction, consequences be damned. It's a good thing everyone has all five needs. Without all five, we may never feel it's possible to prioritize the needs of a relationship over your own.

When you form a relationship worth keeping, what makes it work over the long haul is your collective willingness to prioritize the relationship needs over your own individual needs most of the time.

Learning this simple exercise, The Solving Circle, while you are still choosing to love each other will be invaluable to your relationship. When you and your partner agree to use The Solving Circle Technique, what you are agreeing to, in essence, is prioritizing the needs of your relationship over your personal ones. While operating outside the circle, you are focused more on your individual needs.

To assist you in keeping the focus on the relationship, imagine drawing a protective circle around you and your partner. This should only happen when you and your partner are both prioritizing the needs of the relationship. If one of you is prioritizing your individual needs, then postpone the use of the Solving Circle for a later time when you are both prioritizing the relationship.

If you are prioritizing the relationship, then you agree to step inside this sacred space, the figurative Solving Circle, to listen to the challenge at hand and use the negotiating skills described in Chapter Eight to create a solution that works best for your relationship. You may not create a solution in one attempt. You may need to take a timeout and try again later, but the idea is to never give up. Continue negotiating until you find a solution that works for both of you.

Let's explore an example from an imaginary couple. Sam and Ally have four children. When the kids were small, they both agreed that Ally would stay home with them and put her career on hold. Daycare cost a lot more money than what Ally would earn if she continued to work, and she valued the opportunity to be a stay-at-home mother.

When her youngest child began full-day preschool, Ally wanted to return to work. Sam thought it was too soon. He still thought paying for after-school babysitting would be too expensive and he liked knowing Ally was home with the children.

Individually, Ally wanted to resume her career, while Sam wanted her home with the children still. When Sam accepts Ally's invitation to enter the solving circle, he is agreeing to put the needs of the relationship above his own, as is she. After discussing all the issues, Sam decided he could be home by three in the afternoon, three days a week, if he started working on Saturday. Ally could structure herself to work from home the other two days, provided she could spend a couple hours each night after the kids went to bed getting some work done, too.

As they looked at this solution, they thought it would be best for the relationship, but they worried their time alone as a couple would be compromised, which could damage the relationship over time. Further discussion added Saturday date night and Sunday family time to the plan to maximize the best solution for the relationship.

Ally asked Sam if he was good with the plan. He was. Sam asked the same of Ally and she agreed. It became a win/win/win for the entire family!

10. Happily Ever After

No one gets married thinking divorce is imminent. Typically, when two people get married, they believe that they will live happily ever after. We already know that, at least in the United States, a bit more than half of the couples who get married will also get divorced. Additionally, there are many people who stay married but live in mediocre, or worse, relationships.

In *Secrets of Happy Couples*, I write about people who have the skills they need to obtain the relationship but lack what it takes to maintain the relationship. It's like buying a car and never changing the oil.

Once the newness of a relationship wears off and we start noticing things about our partners we may not like, we start attempting to get them to do what we want them to do—we start to use Disconnecting Relationship Habits. We learn these Disconnecting Habits from our parents, our teachers and other important people in our lives. We learned it from the movies and stories we grew up with. In fact, the entire world seems to embrace the idea of people having the right to force others into doing things they don't want to do, especially if the person decided that it's best for the other person. We convince ourselves that it's our responsibility to get the other person to do what we want.

When referring to imminent physical danger, it may be acceptable to force someone to do something they don't want to do to keep them safe, particularly in the case of children. In all other circumstances, Choice Theory advises to allow everyone to make the choices that they believe are best for their lives. After all, they are the ones who will be living with the consequences.

However, in all other instances, when we use Disconnecting Relationship Habits, it's like we are taking a pick-axe to the very foundation of our relationship. We might be able to hit it without incident several times, but one day, the repeated use of the pick is going to cause a chip. And this chip will one day become a crack. Keep using that pick-axe and, before you realize what is happening, you will see the foundation of your relationship crumble. The Disconnecting Relationship Habits include:

1. Complaining

2. Blaming

3. Criticizing

4. Nagging

5. Threatening

6. Punishing

7. Bribing or rewarding to control

Of course, there are more than seven. People have included guilting, gossiping, discouraging and others in their additions, and I'm sure you can think of even more. It's any behavior we can use to try to control others. If you want a healthy relationship, you will need to become more mindful of these disconnecting behaviors and reduce your use of them.

Proper maintenance behaviors include continuing to do the things you used to do when you were dating, as well as working to stop using Disconnecting Relationship Habits while increasing your use of the Connecting ones:

1. Listening

   This involves listening for understanding as discussed in Chapter Five.

2. Supporting

   Supporting reminds me of the quote by Dr. Martin Luther King, Jr.: "The true measure of a man [or a woman] is not where they stand in times of comfort and convenience, but where they stand in times of challenge and controversy." It's easy to support someone when they are doing what you want, but not so easy when they are doing something that makes things more difficult for you. We need to support the people in our lives, even when it is more difficult for us.

3. Encouraging

Be a cheerleader for the people in your life. Encourage people to do the things they want to do, believe in them until they can believe in themselves and help people bolster their courage to do the things they want to do.

4. Trusting

When someone breaks trust with us, we usually respond in one of two ways. We either become angry or disappointed with the other person for lying and/or breaking a promise, or we become upset with ourselves for being so foolish to trust that person.

When you think of the times you have broken promises, I'll bet you had every intention of keeping it before 'life' got in the way. You didn't lie; you didn't misrepresent yourself. You wanted to honor your word but, unfortunately, you had to reorder your priorities and couldn't do what you planned. I do realize there are people who lie on purpose, but the vast majority of people mean to keep the promises they make, so trust their good intentions, even if they weren't able to follow through.

Sometimes in relationships, we trust people to be who we want to them to be instead of who they've shown us they are. You have a Quality World picture of who you want your partner to be, but many times we connect with people who don't exactly match that picture. And yet, we expect them to be the person we want and follow our script; when they don't, we are disappointed, frustrated and angry. We need to trust our partners to be who they are instead of who we want them to be.

If you want to take trusting to the highest level, then join me in the Unconditional Trust Challenge mentioned in Chapter Seven.

5. Respecting

Respecting in relationships is challenging because we often use what we were taught as children, the Golden Rule: "Do unto others as *you* would have them do onto you." I think this is a great general rule, especially when dealing with people you don't know. However, when you are in a relationship, you may want to engage Tony Alessandro's Platinum Rule: "Do unto others as *they* would have you do unto them."

Our typical behavior is to engage the Golden Rule. You can especially see this in relationships when someone is upset about something. As John Gray wrote in *Men are from Mars; Women are from Venus*, women tend to process externally and men do so internally. Women tend to vent when they're upset, but when a man is listening to venting, he typically responds by offering advice or he leaves her alone so she can work it out in solitude. This is because when a man is upset, he usually isolates until he can figure it out or he calls someone who can fix the problem or help him fix it. And women chase after these men asking them to talk to them and tell them what's wrong. Both are employing the Golden Rule when the Platinum Rule would be best.

6. Accepting

Acceptance is about recognizing that everyone gets one life to live and they are the ones who must live with the consequences of their decisions. I may not like what you choose, but I can accept the fact that you have a right to choose it. Once you do, I have a decision to make about how I want to show up in your life. Maybe I will distance myself from you, move closer, or maintain the status quo. The last thing I would think of is trying to change you or to get you to do something you don't want to do. I accept your right to live your life as you see fit.

7. Negotiating Differences

Being in a relationship, by definition, almost means there *will* be differences. Whenever you are close with another person for extended periods of time, it's inevitable you will want different things at some point. These differences can range from mundane to monumental: disagreeing over what to have for dinner, where to go on a family vacation, or whether to have children.

Going into a negotiation with 'battle mind' is counter-productive unless you are going to war. When you are negotiating with someone important to you, it is best to use the process outlined in Chapter Nine.

Over the years, I've seen many people experience lots of guilt after realizing their use of the Disconnecting Relationship Habits is worse than they thought. This is perfectly natural! We learned them from people we loved, trusted and respected. They did the same, so there's no sense blaming them or anyone who came before.

The best way to reduce your use of the Disconnecting Relationship Habits is to first admit you use them and forgive yourself. Remember the Choice Theory tenet that all people are doing the best they know, with the information available to them, to get something they want at any given point in time. You didn't know, and you can't hold yourself accountable for something you had no knowledge about. Once you accept that, then you will want to forgive others for using external control with you for exactly the same reason. They were doing the best they could with the information available to them.

11. Appreciation Stairway

You usually begin to climb the Appreciation Stairway by starting at the very bottom on the step called Conflict. This is the issue you and your partner have been arguing about. It's been creating difficulty and you don't see each other's point of view at all. When you can clearly visualize a situation that describes this state, ask yourself if you'd like to take a step up the stairway to the next step.

If the answer is no, you'll remain in Conflict—that's always a choice. But if the answer is yes, take a step up to the place called, Toleration. If I'm merely tolerating you, I've made the decision to stop being in conflict with you, but I'm still not happy and I still want you to do something different. I'm frustrated but no longer talking about it. Getting to this step and parking yourself there is not a goal, but it is better than remaining in conflict. At least you are no longer using each other as a virtual punching bag.

Imagine there's another step up. You can climb it or not, the choice is yours. Would you want to move up to the next step? You don't have to, but staying in Toleration does not feel good, still causes stress and you're still putting up with something you do not like. Would you take the next step?

The next step is called Acceptance. The Serenity Prayer was named after this experience and it's used to close many 12-Step Recovery meetings: Grant me the serenity to accept the things I cannot change, the courage to change the things I can and the wisdom to know the difference.

Choice Theory enthusiasts tweak that prayer a bit to say: Grant me the serenity to accept the *people* I cannot change, courage to change the one *I* can and the wisdom to know that person is *me*. In either version, the person is seeking the peace that comes from accepting what can't be changed.

You can decide to accept the thing about your partner that was causing the original conflict. When you look at the entire package that is your partner, is this one thing the make-or-break situation? Chances are there are so many things you love and respect about your partner, but you haven't been able to see them in so long because all you have been doing is living in Conflict.

After reaching Acceptance, most people are quite happy with the results, but there is one more step for those who want to make their relationship even stronger. Do you want to take it? If not, you will live in the place of Acceptance. It's your call — acceptance is not a bad place to be.

However, if you want to climb to the top of the Stairway, then take the last step to Appreciation. You won't regret it. Climbing to Appreciation involves working to recognize that the things you were in conflict over have actually provided something beneficial.

This concept comes from something John Demartini wrote about in *The Breakthrough Experience*. He wrote about the Periodic Table of Elements and how every naturally occurring element in our world is in total balance with an equal number of protons and electrons; there are just as many positive as there are negatively charged particles. From this fact, Demartini extrapolated the concept that life experiences are exactly the same way—equally balanced with positive and negative values.

If this is true, and in my experience I have yet to find an exception, then think of the worst thing that ever happened to you and ask yourself the question, "What is the gift, lesson or opportunity (GLO) in this experience?" You may not immediately have the answer, but know it's there. If you need help finding it, send me an email to kim@therelationshipcenter.biz and I'll see if I can stimulate your thinking in that area. It's challenging because when you've been thinking of something as strictly bad, negative and painful for a long time, it's hard to imagine it being anything else, but that doesn't mean it isn't true.

Are you willing to give it try in your relationship? Think of the area you are in conflict over. Think of your partner's position that's causing you so much anger, frustration, resentment and pain. Then, ask yourself what is the GLO in that conflict for you? Once you can find it, you can end the conflict by appreciating the other person for their part in providing you the GLO.

12. Keeping Your Relationship Strong

As I said before, most people have the knowledge, skills and behaviors they need to obtain the relationship, but it seems no one ever told them about the knowledge, skills and behaviors they would need to maintain the relationship. Thinking your relationship will run on autopilot after the "I do's" is like buying a computer and never running the anti-virus program. It's a recipe for disaster!

How many of the following six suggestions do you use to maintain your relationship?

Platinum Rule

Treat others the way they want to be treated, not the way you would want to be treated. This is a good general practice for all the relationships in your life, but especially for your most intimate one. There are so many variables and situations in which you will want different things: you're an introvert and he's an extrovert, you're liberal and she's conservative, and he values sex while you value romance. Taking the time to think through your options will help you answer the question, "What would my partner want in this situation?" rather than acting from autopilot the way you would want to be treated.

Sex & Romance

In intimacy, there is rarely a problem early in the relationship because there is an abundance of sex and romance. However, as time goes on, these things can diminish. If one of you loves romance and the other loves sex, it creates a challenge when there's a shortage of either one. You try to get more romance by being more romantic with your sexual partner or you try to get more sex by being more sexual with your romantic partner. Employ Alessandro's Platinum Rule. If you want more sex, you need to be more romantic; if you want more romance, you need to be more sexual.

Five Love Languages

In my experience, no one book has been more successful in helping relationships than Gary Chapman's, *5 Love Languages*. Learning your love language and, more importantly, learning and speaking the love language of your partner can really save a diminishing relationship. Chapman helps couples understand that each person has a primary love language that, when spoken, helps them know they are loved. My love language is Quality Time. If you want me to know you love me, you will spend quality time with me—if you know my love language, that is. If you don't, then you will likely speak your love language to me, causing me to misunderstand and probably feel unloved. The other five languages are: Receiving Gifts, Words of

Affirmation, Physical Touch and Acts of Service. Learn your love language here:

www.5lovelanguages.com.

Last Day on Earth

As a widow, it isn't hard to think this way, but I'm suggesting that you ask yourself, "How would I want to treat my partner if I knew today is their last day on earth?" If your answer differs from how you typically treat him or her, then I suggest checking yourself and amending your ways. Everyone has an expiration date and very few of us know the exact day and time. At some point, the next words you are about to say will be the last ones your partner ever hears. Make sure you have no regrets in this department by always speaking with love and kindness to the people you love.

Don't Take it Personally

In relationships, it seems our partners can act as mirrors; we see things in them we don't like in ourselves. When acting in this space without awareness, you or your partner may say things that are hurtful. It will be difficult not to take that personally because it sure feels personal. When you start to feel yourself taking something your partner says personally, stop and talk yourself to a different place: "Wow, I'm really feeling attacked. I guess that means it's my turn to tune in to understand what my partner is trying to communicate. They are in distress right now and even though I might be part of the problem, I know I can also be a part of the solution, so I need to work hard to understand what's happening right now." This may seem impossible right now, but with practice, it can become your go-to behavior.

13. What Do You Do Now?

If you are reading this book, I'll assume that, while you may be doing a lot of the right things for your relationship, there is probably at least one or two things in these pages you could do to improve. Regardless of whether you think your partner has more to do, if there's something you can do, wouldn't you want to do it? Someone needs to take the first step and you are the one with the new information. Are you courageous enough to take the first step? Is this relationship worth it?

In relationships, there are basically three choices. You can change it, accept it, or leave it. Once you leave it, the first two are difficult to achieve. Unless your physical safety is at risk, I suggest you try the first two first. See if changing something you are doing can improve the relationship; if you are the one most unhappy about the relationship, then you are the one with the biggest problem and the responsibility for the solution. How can you act or think differently in order to diminish the problem you are experiencing?

Another option is to accept what is happening. You don't necessarily have to like it or agree, but acceptance means you are giving up your anger, frustration, resentment and attempts to get your partner to do things your way. You realize what they are choosing is the best they can do at this point to get the most of what they want.

Finally, if you find you have made a strong effort to change and the situation hasn't improved, or you learn you just can't accept what is happening or how your partner is at this time, then your best option may be leaving. People may leave physically or emotionally, but when you choose it, you know the door is closed and you do not want to go back.

Some people choose to leave for the 'wrong' reason. They are attempting to manipulate their partner into changing by leaving. I've heard some call it a wake-up call. This is using your absence as a way of externally controlling your partner to do what you want. When you opt to leave, make it because it's what's best for you, not because you are trying to change your partner.

When you give up the need to control your loved ones, you realize there are only three options available to you: change it, accept it, or leave it. Which one will you choose?

14. What If I Don't Have a Relationship?

For those of you who are not in a relationship, I ask, do you want to be?

Single by Choice

If your answer to this question is no, then you have what you want right now and that is a good thing. I suspect some challenges you may experience include the well-intentioned questions of others that ask about your relationship status, perhaps sometimes inferring that there is something 'wrong' with you if you aren't attached to another person in a romantic way.

There is absolutely nothing wrong with being single. In fact, after being married for 17 years, dating for four and then in a long-term relationship for eight, I made the conscious decision to dedicate my life, at this time, to my work. I am very fulfilled and happy doing what I do. I travel, speak with people about life-changing concepts and make amazing friends everywhere I go. I know how to do relationships and I do them well but, right now, I am not interested. I may be again one day, but I am happy and fully satisfied as a single woman.

When I encounter people who seem to feel sorry for me because I'm not in a relationship, I just shake my head and think, if they only knew how happy I am every day, they would not be feeling sorry for me. That's the rub: other people cannot know what is in your heart or your head. They are judging you based on their own standards, values and beliefs. Stand solid in the knowledge that you are living the life you want and allow others the freedom to think what they like about your choices. You are the only one who has to live with those choices.

On the other hand, if you are single and it's the last thing you want to be, are you a person who is between relationships right now or someone who has never really had an intimate relationship?

Between Relationships

If you are the person who is between relationships right now, this can be an amazing time of self-discovery. People who are between relationships can use that time to grieve their former relationship, look at the things to be gleaned from it and prepare for their next one.

Give yourself time to grieve the loss of your last relationship. Some people think it's best to get over a past love by jumping into a rebound relationship, but this only delays the pain, not to mention it is incredibly unfair to your new relationship. It's almost impossible to be the person you want to be in a new relationship when your heart still belongs to your former partner. Take the time you need to work through any feelings you may have of shock, rejection, depression and anger.

When you are ready, start looking for the GLO in the dissolution of that relationship. I know it's there; as painful as the breakup may have been, there is an equal amount of positivity associated with it. Take the time you need to find it so you can be even stronger in your next relationship.

After you have healed yourself, your next step is to write down the traits, qualities, characteristics and behaviors you want your next life partner to have. Place those things into three categories: non-negotiables, important and nice-to-have.

There should only be three to five non-negotiables. Having more is a sign that you are looking for perfection and reasons to exclude people, likely so you can stay safe.

These three to five things are your deal breakers. Here are mine: domestic violence, drug use, smoking and a lack of introspection. When I realize these are part of a person I am dating, or considering dating, I end the relationship. There is no point in continuing a relationship when one of my non-negotiables is being violated. Honoring your non-negotiables can save you a lot of time in the long run.

Much of your list should include those things you really want in a partner. These are mine: likes to travel, can support themselves financially and emotionally, gets along with my children and grandchildren, is proud of me and the work I do, intelligent, spiritual, likes to read, is physically attractive to me, has a high level of integrity and so on. This list can contain as many things as you want in your partner. In fact, the Law of Attraction dictates that the more specific you can be about the person you want in your life, the more likely he or she will show up for you.

Your nice-to-have list includes things that you would appreciate but aren't necessary for the health and satisfaction of your relationship. Some of my nice-to-have qualities are a man who's good with his hands, musically talented and a Democrat. These are not deal-breakers, nor are they qualities that are important to me, but they would be nice.

You have achieved clarity on the next person you want to have in your life. Once you have your lists completed, the last step is the hardest: take a long, hard, honest look at yourself in the mirror and ask yourself, *Am I the person my perfect person would be attracted to?* If you are 50 pounds overweight but keep a non-negotiable dictating your next partner needs to be physically fit, how likely do you think that is going to be? If one of your non-negotiables in no cheating yet you've cheated on everyone you've ever dated, do you think the person you are looking for is going to be interested in you?

When you have identified those areas in yourself that may prevent you from having the successful relationship of your dreams, you have three options: 1. You can keep hoping it will happen, regardless; 2. You can work on transforming yourself into the person who will attract the partner you are seeking; or 3. You can adjust your list to look for someone more realistic for your current lifestyle.

Never Had a Meaningful Relationship

This is a little harder to write about because it depends on the reason why you haven't had a meaningful relationship yet. Has your focus been elsewhere? Do you know where to meet people? Are you shy? Are you insecure? Do you know how to start and keep up conversations? Are you questioning your sexual orientation? Are you protecting yourself from rejection and pain? Are you fearful you will screw it all up?

All of these and more could be reasons for not having relationships in your life up to this point. People don't change until the pain of staying the same exceeds their fear of change. I'm not going to tell you this will be easy. It could be but, most likely, it's going to be a challenge that requires a lot of commitment and work.

You are single for a reason, maybe several reasons, so it's been working for you. Perhaps, it's been working for you for a very long time. The first question to ask yourself is whether you *really* want a relationship in your life.

If that answer is yes, then the next question is are you willing to do whatever it takes to make that happen, even if it involves rejection, pain and fear?

If your answer to this question is yes, then determine what your current behaviors are for getting a date. I know people who are interested in dating but they never leave their homes and aren't on any dating sites. They may be waiting for the Uber Eats delivery person as their next date, but, otherwise, their dating options are slim.

I am not recommending heading to the clubs or the gym in search of your perfect mate. I am suggesting that you live your life. Engage with life, do the things you like and meet with the people you most enjoy. Pay attention those you meet at your regular activities. If you are involved in activities where there isn't ever anyone remotely attractive to you, then expose yourself to new things. Do not go 'hunting' for your person, but allow the Universe to put him or her on your path. However, you must do your part… you need to be on a path.

If there are things you are lacking, such as conversational ability, confidence and trust — practice. Search for role models in real life, books or the big screen. Study the people who are good at what you lack and emulate them. Practice, practice, practice. You can only get better. Know that there is very little you can't do if you want it badly enough and are willing to put in the required effort to get there. No one said it would be easy or simple. Keep remembering your reason for wanting a relationship and don't give up. You will likely make some new friends along the way; be open to whatever form your relationships take until you find the one that's right for you.

Relationships and love are the things that can make life worth living. They can provide shelter during challenging times, celebration in good times, a witness to your own life and someone to walk a similar path with. Relationships can come for a reason, a season or a lifetime. Be grateful for them all, learn from them and always be open for what happens next.

Further Exercises

Need-strength Assessment - If you would like to discover the strength of each of your needs, please visit The Relationship Center and take each assessment. The needs are labeled a little differently: Love & Belonging is Connection, Power is Significance and Fun is Joy. Freedom and Survival are the same. You will find them at

www.therelationshipcenter.biz/resources.

5 Problem-Solving Questions: Ask, Answer, Analyze: You have learned the concept of "Structured Reality Therapy." but you haven't yet experienced the process of Reality Therapy. Reality Therapy was developed by Dr. William Glasser in 1965 and consists of a series of five basic questions that can help people decide what to do next. Whenever you are struggling with a challenge, whether a relationship challenge or something else, ask yourself the following questions. Ask them, answer them and analyze the results to determine your next best course of action.

1. What do I want? This question asks you to ponder the situation at hand and determine what you are hoping for in the outcome. When you begin using this process, you may find a lot of what you

want is for other people to do something different. While it is fine to ask people to change what they are doing to suit you, it doesn't always happen that way. If it does, great! However, most people are doing what they do to because it's working for them. After asking, especially after asking the third time, you might want to accept that the other person isn't going to fix whatever problem you are having. So then, you then need to ask yourself, what do you want from the situation if this person doesn't change? Sometimes the answer to this question is that you want to be the person you are even in difficult situations. Sometimes the information you get from other people necessitates an action on your part, such as drawing a boundary, changing what you have been doing or accepting the reality of your situation. While your answer to this question may start as something you want from someone else, it often works its way back to your responsibility for changing the things you are unhappy about. What do you want to have, do or be differently at the end of the process?

2. *What are you doing to get what you want?* This question asks you to examine all the things are you already doing, which includes both the things that are helping and the things that may be preventing you from obtaining your desired outcome. You can include not

only the behaviors you are using, but also your beliefs and what you've been thinking about it, your emotions around what is happening and your body's response to it. They are all connected. Some of it helps you, and some hurts you. An example might be the woman who wants a loving relationship with her husband but she is very insecure and often jealous of work relationships he has with women. When she looks at what she is doing, thinking and feeling, she realizes her behavior may be the very thing that pushes her husband away. Her choices are counterproductive to her goal. Does this happen with you sometimes?

3. *Is it working?* This is when you take an honest appraisal of the situation to see if what you are doing is likely to lead to your desired outcome. If the answer is yes, wonderful! If the answer is no, you have choices to make. Will you continue on your ill-fated path or choose to do something different? When you complete this evaluation of your current behavior, your answer may be that you don't know if it's working or maybe it's working, but too slowly. In these situations, you will need to assess if you want to change your actions, increase what you are doing or continue your same path until you have more information. It is also important to

mention responsibility. If you determine what you're doing is working but it may be against the rules, against the law or might hurt someone, including yourself, then you need to add another question: *Am I willing to risk the consequences of my behavior or do I want to work to find a solution that can get me what I want without breaking the rules, breaking the law or hurting anyone?*

4. *Are you willing to do something different?* This is where you assess your motivation and determination to take a different path. It isn't always an easy thing to try something new. It can feel scary and uncertain. However, if you can plainly see what you are doing is taking you down the wrong path, it might seem ludicrous to continue in the same vein.

5. *Make a plan.* This is the step where you decide exactly what you are going to do. You may decide to continue exactly the way you have been or you may choose something different. Either way, you commit to your path and the steps necessary to move you in the direction of your goal.

Using this questioning process can help you make better, rational decisions. One word of caution, if what you want in the first question is unattainable, you may want to rethink your goal. There is nothing more painful than wanting something you can't have; it sentences you to a lifetime of misery and unhappiness. When what you want is something that isn't possible, ask yourself which of your needs (Survival, Love & Belonging, Power, Freedom and Fun) would be met if you were able to have it. Once you have identified the need or needs underlying that desire, you can make a plan to get more of the need met in your life, even if it can't be met the way you prefer. It's like the Rolling Stones sang, "You can't always get what you want, but if you try sometimes, you just might find, you'll get what you need."

Love and the desire for relationships are part of being human. We are relational beings. There doesn't seem to be a shortage of people connecting with partners. The beauty comes from honoring someone enough to make a life with that person, but it requires effort and skills. Hopefully, this book has equipped you with some extra tools to make your next relationship a good one.

Bibliography

Olver, K. (2019). *Choosing Me Now: Letting go of what doesn't work to make room for what does.* Chicago: InsideOut Press.

Olver, K. (2011). *Secrets of Happy Couples: Loving yourself, your partner and your life.* Chicago: InsideOut Press.

Olver, K. (2006). *Leveraging Diversity at Work: How to hire, retain and inspire a diverse workforce for peak performance and profit.* Chicago: InsideOut Press.

Chapman, G. (1992). *The 5 Love Languages: The secret to love that lasts.* Chicago: Northfield Publishing.

Covey, S. R. (1989). *The 7 Habits of Highly Effective People: Powerful lessons in personal change.* New York: Simon & Schuster.

Demartini, J. (2002). *The Breakthrough Experience: A revolutionary new approach to personal transformation.* New York: Hay House, Inc.

Glasser, W. (1998). *Choice Theory: A new psychology of personal freedom.* New York: HarperCollins.

Glasser, W. (2007). *Eight Lessons for a Happier Marriage.* New York: HarperCollins.

Glasser, C. &Glasser, W. (2000). *Getting Together and Staying Together: Solving the mystery of marriage.* New York: HarperCollins.

Gray, J. (1992). *Men are from Mars, Women are from Venus: A practical guide for improving communication and getting what you want in your relationships.* New York: HarperCollins.

The Choice Theory in Action Series Titles

A Choice Theory Psychology Guide to Addictions: Ways to Overcome Substance Dependence and Other Compulsive Behaviors - Michael Rice

A Choice Theory Psychology Guide to Anger Management: How to Manage Rage in Your Life - Brian Lennon

A Choice Theory Psychology Guide to Depression: Lift Your Mood - Robert E. Wubbolding, Ph.D.

A Choice Theory Psychology Guide to Happiness: How to Make Yourself Happy - Carleen Glasser

A Choice Theory Psychology Guide to Parenting: The Art of Raising Great Children - Nancy S. Buck Ph.D.

A Choice Theory Psychology Guide to Relationships: How to Get Along with the Important People in Your Life - Kim Olver

A Choice Theory Psychology Guide to Stress: Ways of Managing Stress in Your Life - Brian Lennon

The Choice Theory in Action Series is available from Amazon as e-books or paperbacks and may be obtained through bookshops including wglasserbooks.com

William Glasser International

The body that Dr. Glasser approved to continue teaching and developing his ideas is William Glasser International.

This organization helps coordinate the work of many member organizations around the world.

WGI recently introduced a six-hour workshop entitled, "Taking Charge of Your Life". This is intended for the general public and provides a good foundation in Choice Theory psychology.

If you are interested in further training in Choice Theory psychology or any of its applications, you are recommended to contact WGI or your nearest member organization of WGI.

www.wglasserinternational.org

William Glasser International
4053 W 183rd Place, #2666
Country Club Hills, IL 60478, U.S.A.

Phone: +1 708-957-6048
Fax: +1 708-957-8028
Email: wgi@wglasserinternational.org

Made in the USA
Lexington, KY
31 July 2019